NFL TEAM STORIES

THE STORY OF THE

BUFFALO BILLS

By Mark and Solomon Shulman

Kaleidoscope
Minneapolis, MN

Bigfoot Books

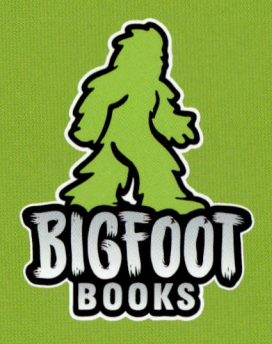

The Quest for Discovery Never Ends

This edition first published in 2021 by Kaleidoscope Publishing, Inc.

No part of this publication may be reproduced in whole or in part without written permission of the publisher.

For information regarding permission, write to
Kaleidoscope Publishing, Inc.
6012 Blue Circle Drive
Minnetonka, MN 55343

Library of Congress Control Number
2020933488

ISBN
978-1-64519-221-3 (library bound)
978-1-64519-289-3 (ebook)

Text copyright © 2021 by Kaleidoscope Publishing, Inc. All-Star Sports, Bigfoot Books, and associated logos are trademarks and/or registered trademarks of Kaleidoscope Publishing, Inc.

Printed in the United States of America.

FIND ME IF YOU CAN!

Bigfoot lurks within one of the images in this book. It's up to you to find him!

TABLE OF CONTENTS

Kickoff! 4

Chapter 1: Bills History 6

Chapter 2: Bills All-Time Greats 16

Chapter 3: Bills Superstars 22

Beyond the Book 28
Research Ninja 29
Further Resources 30
Glossary 31
Index 32
Photo Credits 32
About the Author 32

KICKOFF!

Who's in that wave of red and blue? Who's cheering so loud other teams can't hear? Who wears chicken wing hats? It's the super fans of the Buffalo Bills!

Buffalo stands by their Bills, in the best times and the worst weather. Bills players win big in Buffalo's wind and snow. The other teams freeze up. Bills fans bring warm clothes and blankets. They cheer to the very end. Winning makes everyone warm!

Let's go, Buffalo!

FUN FACT
The coldest game ever in Buffalo was 0°F (−18°C)!

Chapter 1
Bills History

A businessman named Ralph Wilson wanted a football team. In 1960, he helped start a new league called the American Football League (AFL). Wilson's Buffalo Bills were one of the AFL's eight teams.

The Bills were strong from the start. Coach Lou Saban and quarterback Jack Kemp led the Bills. The team won the AFL in 1964 and 1965. That's like winning back-to-back Super Bowls. Buffalo was on its way!

In the 1970s, the Bills played in an old baseball stadium. Fans called it "The Rock Pile." A new football stadium was built in 1973. It was a new start for the Bills.

Pete Gogolak (3), Jack Kemp (15), and Wray Carlton (30) celebrate after the Bills won the AFL title in 1964.

In the 1980s, a new coach, Marv Levy, set up a powerful Bills roster. With QB Jim Kelly, they played a quick new way. They rarely stopped for a huddle. Kelly moved the ball so fast, other teams could not keep up. They called this the "No-Huddle Offense." Why was this new? Few teams did it! Doing something new and different made the Bills winners.

In 1988, they won the AFC East title for the second time. It was the start of a great run of success in Buffalo.

"Okay, guys, here's the next play! Get ready!"

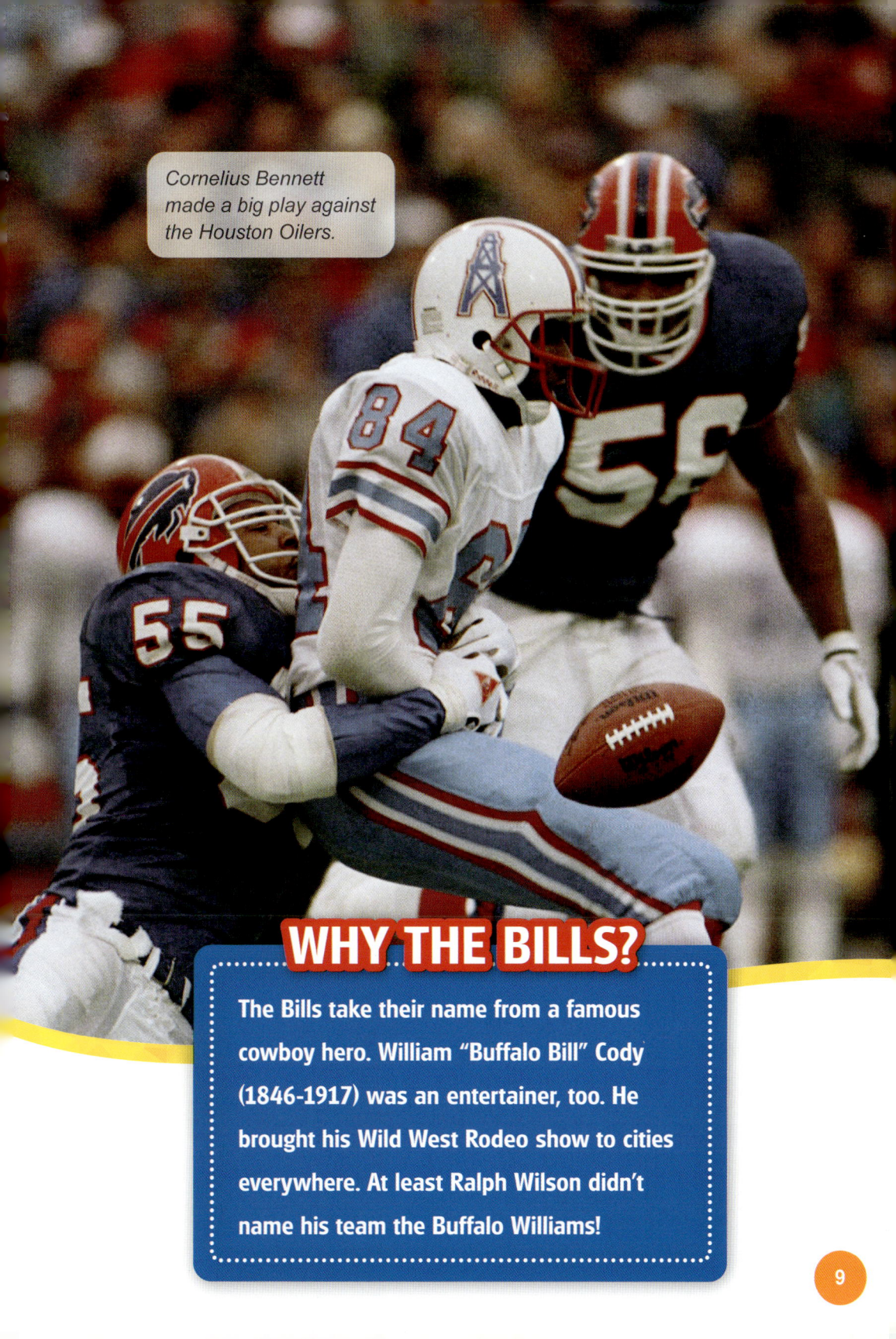

Cornelius Bennett made a big play against the Houston Oilers.

WHY THE BILLS?

The Bills take their name from a famous cowboy hero. William "Buffalo Bill" Cody (1846-1917) was an entertainer, too. He brought his Wild West Rodeo show to cities everywhere. At least Ralph Wilson didn't name his team the Buffalo Williams!

From 1990 to 1993, the Buffalo Bills were one of the NFL's best teams. They won four AFC Championship Games in a row. That put them in four straight Super Bowls!

Super Bowl XXV was the closest title game ever played. The score was 20-19. The Bills never came closer. They lost the next three Super Bowls. In one of them, a Bills player made a famous play. It was Super Bowl XXVII. Leon Lett of the Cowboys picked up a **fumble**. He headed for the end zone. Buffalo's Don Beebe didn't give up. He raced 60 yards after Lett. Beebe knocked the ball away just before Lett scored. Bills fans were proud of him!

FUN FACT

The Bills are the only team to play in four straight Super Bowls.

Beebe's hustle kept the Cowboys from scoring.

In 1998 and 1999, QB Doug Flutie led the Bills back to the playoffs. Flutie was small but quick. He was so popular, they named a cereal after him. It was called Flutie Flakes!

The Bills struggled in the 2000s. They had only two **winning seasons** from 2000 to 2016. Bills fans froze, but they stuck with their team. It was worth the wait.

In 2017, new coach Sean McDermott led them back to the playoffs. The next year, **rookie** QB Josh Allen arrived. He brought size, speed, and power. The Bills went back to the playoffs again in 2019.

Buffalo fans can feel the excitement!

FUN FACT

Josh Allen had 30 TD passes in his first 28 NFL games.

QB Josh Allen

TIMELINE OF THE BUFFALO BILLS

1960
1960: The Buffalo Bills started play.

1965
1965: Bills win second AFL championship in a row.

1990
1990: Bills reach Super Bowl XXV, the team's first.

1993
1993: Bills set record with fourth Super Bowl in a row.

1999
1999: Bills reach the playoffs under QB Doug Flutie.

2017
2017: Bills hire young coach Sean McDermott.

2019
2019: Bills return to second playoffs in three seasons.

THE GREATEST COMEBACK EVER!

In a 1992 playoff game, the Bills were in trouble. QB Jim Kelly was hurt. To return to the Super Bowl, they had to win. The Bills fell way behind the Houston Oilers, 28–3. Then, the second half started. Oh, no! Houston got a pick six. Buffalo was now behind by 32 points—35–3.

But the Bills never gave up. In 20 minutes, backup QB Frank Reich threw three touchdowns. That made the game closer. Buffalo was behind 35–24. Then the Bills scored two more times! Kicker Steve Christie made a field goal to give Buffalo a 38–35 lead.

It wasn't over yet.

Houston came back to tie the score. That meant overtime!

In the OT, Christie kicked another field goal and the Bills won 41–38. They soon went to the Super Bowl!

The Bills had rallied from 32 points behind. Their win is still the greatest comeback in NFL playoff history!

Chapter 2
Bills All-Time Greats

Jack Kemp was the first great Bills QB. His powerful arm led the young Bills to two AFL titles in a row. Kemp set the Bills record for passing yards. He also ran for a lot of touchdowns. After football, Kemp was elected to the United States Congress.

Jim Kelly came along to break Kemp's records. This hard-working passer led the Bills to the playoffs eight times. He is the only NFL QB to start in four straight Super Bowls.

O.J. Simpson was Buffalo's star running back. He was fast and hard to tackle. Simpson was the first NFL player to run more than 2,000 yards in a season. Only six players have ever done this. Simpson is the only one to do it in just 14 games.

FUN FACT

Jim Kelly was elected to the Pro Football Hall of Fame in 2002.

Thurman Thomas

Thurman Thomas was the best all-around back Buffalo ever had. He could cut through tight defenses. He could catch long passes. He could run up the middle. And he always made it look easy. Thomas ran for almost 12,000 yards, and caught 456 passes with the Bills. It was a Hall of Fame career!

Andre Reed was a fast and graceful wide receiver. He had the power to push past a defender. In 15 years with the Bills, Reed caught 941 passes and scored 87 touchdowns. This Hall of Famer made seven trips to the Pro Bowl. That's the NFL all-star game.

Andre Reed

Buffalo's fans chanted "*Brooooo!*" They weren't booing. They loved Bruce Smith. But quarterbacks feared him. They called this tall and powerful defensive end "Sack Man." With blinding speed, Smith would slip past any blockers. Smith owns the NFL record with exactly 200 **sacks**. This Hall of Fame Bruce was on the loose!

FUN FACT

Smith was named to the NFL's All-Decade Team for the 1990s.

Bruce Smith

BILLS RECORDS

These players piled up the best stats in Bills history. The numbers are career records through the 2019 season.

Total TDs: Andre Reed/Thurman Thomas, 87

TD Passes: Jim Kelly, 237

Passing Yards: Jim Kelly, 35,467

Receiving Yards: Andre Reed, 13,095

Rushing Yards: Thurman Thomas, 11,938

Receptions: Andre Reed, 941

Points: Steve Christie, 1,011

Sacks: Bruce Smith, 171

Chapter 3
Bills Superstars

Quarterback Josh Allen was the Bills first-round draft pick in 2018. The team wanted him to become the leader. He didn't wait long! Allen became the **starter** five games into the season. Since then, he had led the Bills to many big wins. In 2019, his passing and running carried them into the playoffs. His 17 rushing touchdowns in two seasons were second most among all NFL quarterbacks.

HEAVE IT!

Josh Allen can throw the football more than 80 yards. That's more than eight school buses parked end-to-end! In just two years, Allen passed for more than 5,000 yards. That's almost three miles!

Josh Allen dives for a touchdown against the Houston Texans.

23

The Bills have one of the best defenses in the NFL. They give up very few points. One reason is cornerback Tre'Davious White. He can think fast and read plays before they happen. The ball is passed. The receiver is ready. But White jumps high and takes it. **Interception**! White steals the ball again!

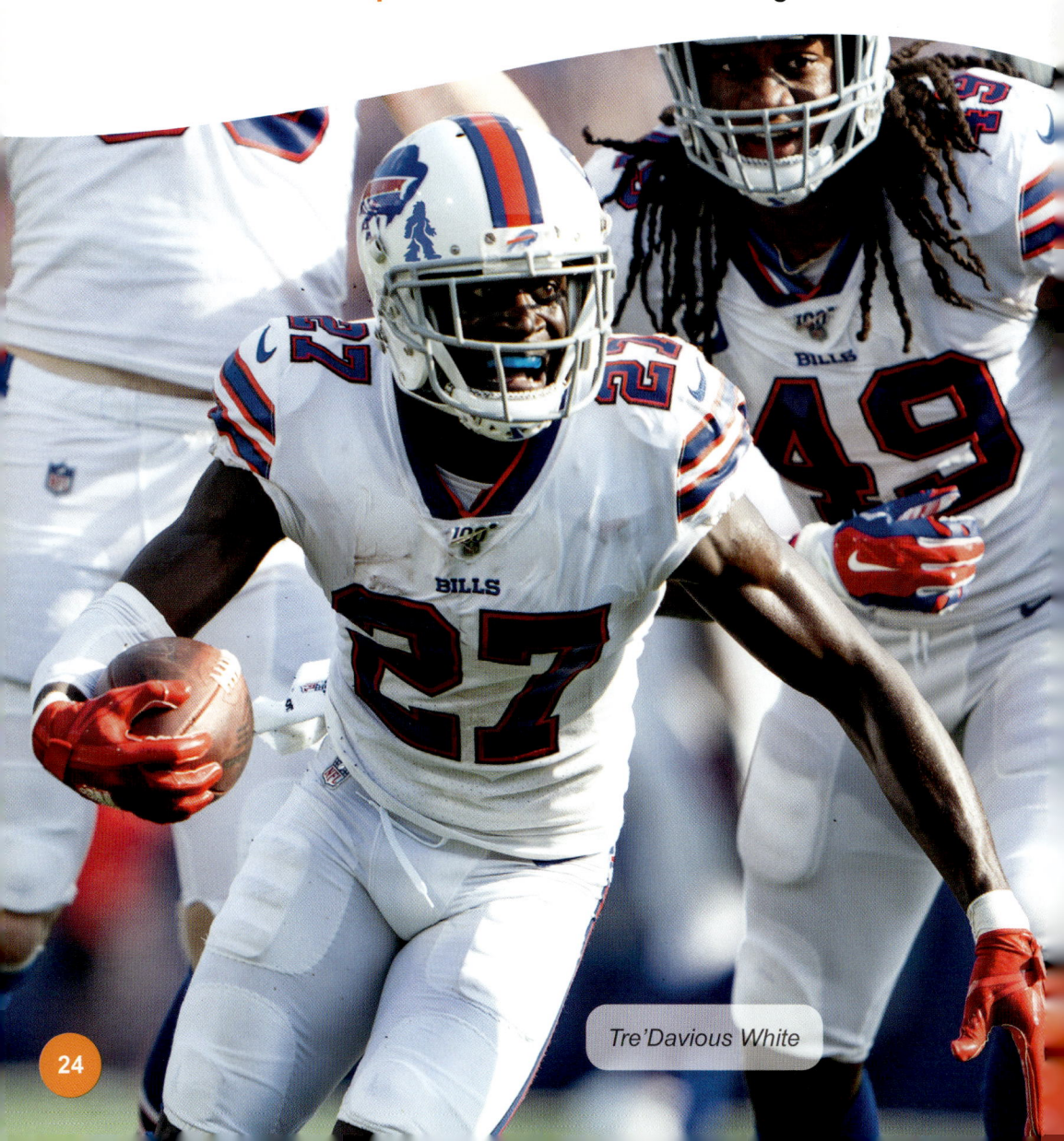

Tre'Davious White

Jordan Phillips

Young linebacker Tremaine Edmunds made the Pro Bowl for the first time in 2019. He led the team with 115 tackles. He was a big reason Buffalo had the No. 3 defense in the NFL.

Josh Allen has help on offense. In 2019, running back Devin Singletary had a great rookie year. He has quick moves. He leaves other teams in the dust. Singletary did well both running and catching the ball. Buffalo has high hopes for him to keep getting better.

John Brown joined the Bills in 2019. In 2019, he made 72 catches, the most of his career. Brown also scored six touchdowns. Then the team added star receiver Stefon Diggs in a big trade in 2020. His best year came when he caught 102 passes for Minnesota in 2018.

With a great young passer and a strong defense, the Bills are ready to stampede back to the Super Bowl!

Devin Singletary takes on the Pittsburgh Steelers.

BEYOND
THE BOOK

After reading the book, it's time to think about what you learned.
Try the following exercises to jumpstart your ideas.

RESEARCH

FIND OUT MORE. Where would you go to find out more about your favorite NFL teams and players? Check out NFL.com, of course. Each team also has its own website. What other sports information sites can you find? See if you can find other cool facts about your favorite team.

CREATE

GET ARTISTIC. Each NFL team has a logo. The Bills logo shows a big buffalo! Get some art materials and try designing your own Bills logo. Or create a new team and make a logo for it. What colors would you choose? How would you draw the mascot?

DISCOVER

GO DEEP! As this book shows, the Bills lost four Super Bowls . . . in a row! That must have been hard for fans. Think about how you would feel if your team got so close so often, but didn't win. Would you still root for them? How would you stay positive even though disappointed?

GROW

GET OUT AND PLAY! You don't need to be in the NFL to enjoy football. You just need a football and some friends. Play touch or tag football. Or you can hang cloth flags from your belt; grab the belt and make the "tackle." See who has the best arm to be quarterback. Who is the best receiver? Who can run the fastest? Time to play football!

RESEARCH NINJA

Visit **www.ninjaresearcher.com/2213** to learn how to take your research skills and book report writing to the next level!

RESEARCH

DIGITAL LITERACY TOOLS

SEARCH LIKE A PRO
Learn about how to use search engines to find useful websites.

FACT OR FAKE?
Discover how you can tell a trusted website from an untrustworthy resource.

TEXT DETECTIVE
Explore how to zero in on the information you need most.

SHOW YOUR WORK
Research responsibly—learn how to cite sources.

WRITE

GET TO THE POINT
Learn how to express your main ideas.

PLAN OF ATTACK
Learn prewriting exercises and create an outline.

DOWNLOADABLE REPORT FORMS

Further Resources

BOOKS

Cooper, Robert. *Great Moments in NFL History*. Minneapolis: North Star Editions, 2019.

Football: Then to Wow! New York: Sports Illustrated Kids, 2014.

Whiting, Jim. *Buffalo Bills*. Mankato, Minn.: Creative Paperbacks, 2019.

WEBSITES

FACTSURFER

Factsurfer.com gives you a safe, fun way to find more information.

1. Go to www.factsurfer.com.
2. Enter "Buffalo Bills " into the search box and click 🔍
3. Select your book cover to see a list of related websites.

Glossary

backup: a player who is ready to replace a starter. Josh Allen's backup is Matt Barkley.

fumble: to drop the ball while carrying it. Buffalo recovered a big fumble by their opponent's running back.

interception: a pass caught by the other team. Tre'Davious White leaped to make an interception of a Steelers pass.

overtime: extra time played when a 60-minute NFL game ends in a tie. The Bills needed overtime to complete their big comeback.

pick six: an interception returned for a touchdown. Levi Wallace raced to the end zone for a pick six.

rookie: a player in his first pro season. Josh Allen threw 10 TD passes in 2017, his rookie season.

roster: the list of players on the team. The Bills have five running backs on their roster.

sacks: tackles made of the quarterback behind the line of scrimmage. The sack by Bruce Smith pushed the Patriots back nine yards.

starter: a player who begins the game in his team's lineup. Jim Kelly was the Bills starter at quarterback for 11 seasons.

winning season: a year in which a team wins more than it loses. With 10 wins and 6 losses, the Bills had a winning season.

Index

Allen, Josh, 12, 22, 26
American Football League (AFL), 6, 16
Beebe, Don, 10
Brown, John, 26
Christie, Steve, 15
Cody, William "Buffalo Bill," 9
Dallas Cowboys, 10
Diggs, Stefon, 26
Edmunds, Tremaine, 25
Flutie, Doug, 12
Houston Oilers, 14, 15
Kelly, Jim, 8, 14, 16
Kemp, Jack, 6, 16
Lett, Leon, 10
Levy, Marv, 8
McDermott, Sean, 12
"No-Huddle Offense," 8
Reed, Andre, 19
Reich, Frank, 15
Saban, Lou, 6
Simpson, O.J., 16
Singletary, Devin, 26
Smith, Bruce, 20
Super Bowl, 6, 10, 14, 15, 16, 26
Thomas, Thurman, 18
White, Tre'Davious, 24
Wilson, Ralph, 6, 9

PHOTO CREDITS

The images in this book are reproduced through the courtesy of: AP Photos: Adrian Kraus 4; 6; NFL Photo 8, 10; Mike Groll 9; John Hickey 14; Chuck Solomon 15; Four Seam Images 19. Focus on Football: 12; 20, 26. Newscom: Cliff Welch/Icon SMI 18; Ken Murray/Icon SW 22; Gregory Fisher/Icon SW 24; Joshua Sarner/Icon SW 25. **Cover photo:** Focus on Football.

About the Author

Mark and Solomon Shulman are a writing team with more than 150 books for young readers between them. They are based in New York City, yet they love no team more than the Buffalo Bills.